CHILDREN LIKE US

Schools

AROUND THE WORLD

Moira Butterfield

Cavendish Square
New York

Published in 2016 by Cavendish Square Publishing, LLC
243 5th Avenue, Suite 136, New York, NY 10016

Website: cavendishsq.com

This publication represents the opinions and views of the author based on his or her personal experience, knowledge, and research. The information in this book serves as a general guide only. The author and publisher have used their best efforts in preparing this book and disclaim liability rising directly or indirectly from the use and application of this book.

CPSIA Compliance Information: Batch #CW16CSQ

All websites were available and accurate when this book was sent to press.However, it is possible that contents or addresses may have changed since the publication of this book. No responsibility for any such changes can be accepted by either the author or the Publisher.

Cataloging-in-Publication Data

Butterfield, Moira.
Schools around the world / by Moira Butterfield.
p. cm. — (Children like us)
Includes index.
ISBN 978-1-5026-0848-2 (hardcover) ISBN 978-1-5026-0846-8 (paperback) ISBN 978-1-5026-0849-9 (ebook)
1. Schools — Juvenile literature. 2. Children — Cross-cultural studies — Juvenile literature.
3. Education — Cross-cultural studies — Juvenile literature. I. Butterfield, Moira, 1960-. II. Title.
LB1513.B88 2016
371—d23

Editor: Izzi Howell
Designer: Clare Nicholas
Picture researcher: Izzi Howell
Proofreaders: Izzi Howell/Stephen White-Thomson
Wayland editor: Annabel Stones

Picture credits:
The author and publisher would like to thank the following for allowing their pictures to be reproduced in this publication: cover Zurijeta/Shutterstock.com; p.3 (t-b) Britta Kasholm-Tengve/The author and publisher would like to thank the following for allowing their pictures to be reproduced in this publication: cover TK; p.3 (t-b) Aleksandar Todorovic/Shutterstock, demerzel21/iStock, Gail Palethorpe/Shutterstock, Vikram Raghuvanshi/iStock; pp.4-5 (c) ekler/Shutterstock; p.4 (t) Christopher Futcher/iStock, (b) ajman33/iStock; p.5 (tl) Dominik Pabis/iStock, (tr) li jianbing/Shutterstock, (br) nguyenkhacthanh/Shutterstock; p.6 (t) DavorLovincic/iStock, (c) Dominik Pabis/iStock, (b) Frederic Soltan/Corbis; p.7 EdStock/iStock; p.8 epa/Corbis; p.9 (t) danishkhan/iStock, (b) Bill Bachman / Alamy; p.10 (t) demerzel21/iStock, (b) nguyenkhacthanh/Shutterstock; p.11 Hugh Sitton/Corbis; p.12 (tr) Grigvovan/Shutterstock, (bl) Aaron Huey/National Geographic Creative/Corbis, (br) egorovnick/Shutterstock; p.13 Radius Images/Corbis; p.14 (tl) BartCo/iStock, (cr) Hugh Sitton/Corbis, (bl) ajman33/iStock; p.15 Ton Koene/Visuals Unlimited/Corbis; p.16 (tr) Tomas van Houtryve/VII/Corbis, (bl) Vikram Raghuvanshi/iStock, (br) Bartosz Hadyniak/iStock; p.17 Thierry Tronnel/Corbis; p.18 (tl) xPACIFICA/Corbis, (cl) bruniewska/iStock, (br) Christopher Futcher/iStock; p.19 Sanjeev Gupta/epa/Corbis; p.20 (tr) pamspix/iStock, (cr) Karen Kasmauski/Corbis, (bl) Studio-Annika/iStock; p.21 Tuul & Bruno Morandi/Corbis; p.22 (t) Dougal Thomas/Corbis, (b) li jianbing/Shutterstock; p.23 Gideon Mendel/In Pictures/Corbis; p.24 Thomas Mukoya/Reuters/Corbis; p.25 (t) Gail Palethorpe/Shutterstock, Baciu/Shutterstock; p.26 (tr) Aaron Huey/National Geographic Creative/Corbis, (bl and br) Necip Yanmaz/iStock; p.27 Randy Olson/National Geographic Creative/Corbis; p.28 (tr) Fritz Hoffmann/In Pictures/Corbis, (bl) idome/Shutterstock, (br) Aleksandar Todorovic/Shutterstock; p.29 Krishnendu Halder/Reuters/Corbis; p.30 (l-r, t-b) idome/Shutterstock, bruniewska/iStock, Christopher Futcher/iStock, Necip Yanmaz/iStock, Studio-Annika/iStock, EdStock/iStock, li jianbing/Shutterstock, pamspix/iStock, Baciu/Shutterstock, danishkhan/iStock, BartCo/iStock, Grigvovan/Shutterstock, Bartosz Hadyniak/iStock; p.31 (l) ajman33/iStock, (r) nguyenkhacthanh/Shutterstock.

Design elements used throughout: Moofer/Shutterstock, rassco/Shutterstock, lilac/Shutterstock, gladcov/Shutterstock, Matthew Cole/Shutterstock, Dacian G/Shutterstock, Malchev/Shutterstock, sommthink/Shutterstock, Studio Barcelona/Shutterstock, katarina_1/Shutterstock, Popmarleo/Shutterstock, Divergenta/Shutterstock, Spreadthesign/Shutterstock, Juli Hansen/Shutterstock, VikaSuh/Shutterstock, Ingka D. Jiw/Shutterstock.

Printed in the United States of America

Contents

All Kinds of Schools

Children around the world go to school just like you. You'll learn about schools in busy cities and tiny villages. You'll discover different kinds of classrooms and school clothes, too.

Find out what sport these American children are doing on page 18.

Find out about this Peruvian boy's school hat on page 14.

Find out what game these Chinese girls are playing at recess on page 22.

Discover how these Indian girls get to their school on page 6.

Can you guess why these Vietnamese schoolchildren have lessons outside? Find out why on page 10.

Take a journey around the world to discover the schools of children just like you!

Off to School

In Asian countries, children in cities often take a rickshaw or *tuk-tuk* to school. These small vehicles can weave their way though traffic. No one wants to be late for school. Rickshaws and *tuk-tuks* are often piled high with children.

A *tuk-tuk* is a three-wheeled motorbike taxi.

A rickshaw is a three-wheeled bike used as a taxi.

Many city children take the subway to school. It is often quicker than driving through the crowded streets. These children are taking the subway in Tokyo, Japan.

These Japanese children are carrying their school books in a backpack called a *randoseru*.

The children of Gulucun live high above a steep canyon in China. To get to school, they walk along a narrow mountain path. Some of the children walk for three hours to get to school.

The path these Chinese children take to school is nearly 1 mile (1500 m) up.

Big Schools, Small Schools

The world's biggest school is the City Montessori School. It is in Lucknow, India. When the school first started, it had five pupils. Today, the school has 47,000 pupils! The school's one-thousand classrooms are spread across the city.

On Children's Day, all the students and teachers at the world's largest school celebrate together.

The Street School in Lyari, Pakistan, is so small that it doesn't even have a building. Instead, it's run in a curtained-off corner of a busy street. At first, the curtain was made from old flour bags. The children sat on the ground. Today, the school has more equipment.

The Street School, pictured here, was set up in 1985 to teach poor children.

School of the Air students talk to their teachers with video cameras and microphones.

This Australian girl is the only student in her class! She's studying with the School of the Air. She lives a long way from the nearest school. Students living in the outback use computers to attend the School of the Air.

Schools in Hot Places

In tropical places, it can be very warm and rainy. This outdoor classroom in eastern Ghana has a roof to keep the rain out. There are no walls, though. This lets cooling air move through.

This classroom in Ghana has its own natural air conditioning.

This classroom is completely outdoors. In Yen Bai, Vietnam, class is held outside in summer. The children go back inside the school in winter when it's rainy and cold.

The children at this Vietnamese school move their desks and benches outside in summer.

These children live in a village in the Amazon rain forest in Ecuador, South America. Their school building is a grass hut. It has open sides and a dirt floor. It was built using dried plants from the rain forest.

These Ecuadorian children learn in a classroom with a roof made of dried grasses.

C SINH TÍCH CỰC!

Schools in Cold Places

This school in Tver, Russia, has a wood-burning fireplace in the classroom. Winters are snowy and cold in Tver. The fire is kept burning throughout the school day.

This Russian schoolgirl has found a warm spot near the fireplace.

Ushguli is the highest community in Europe. It sits among high, snowy mountains in Georgia. The children play inside during recess because it's cold and snowy outdoors.

These Georgian schoolchildren keep their coats on in school to stay warm.

The villages in Ushguli are covered in snow for six months of the year.

These Norwegian children are skiing with their teacher.

In winter, all schools in Norway have something called Ski Day. On this day, students go outside to learn skiing for the day. Norwegian children often begin learning to ski at around age three.

School Clothes

The children in this Malaysian school are Muslims. For religious reasons, the girls cover their heads with a long headscarf. The girls also wear long-sleeved tunics and skirts. The boys wear round caps.

These school uniforms are based on traditional Muslim clothing.

Quechua children wear warm clothes to school. This girl wears a wool jacket and hat. The Quechua live high in the Andes Mountains in South America.

To keep warm, this boy from Peru is wearing a wool hat that he knit himself.

This Quechua girl is wearing a jacket made from llama or alpaca wool.

The Xingu people often draw patterns on their faces.

This boy is sitting in a village school near the Xingu River in the Brazilian Amazon. At his school, they don't wear uniforms. They are allowed to wear their everyday clothing in class. His headdress is made from parrot feathers.

How We Learn

In some schools, children use technology to learn. Instead of blackboards, teachers can use electronic whiteboards to show their students websites and videos. Students use laptops or tablets, too.

In this South Korean school, a robot puppy plays educational games with the children.

These children are learning in a village school in Ratnagiri, India. Their classroom doesn't have chairs or desks. The children sit on soft rugs. Their teacher is using chalk to write on a blackboard.

These Indian schoolchildren learn by reading from a blackboard.

This Ethiopian girl writes on the blackboard.

These Chinese children do not have money for modern learning tools.

These boys carry abacuses to school. The abacuses have beads that will help them do math. The boys belong to the Nakhi community. They live in the foothills of the Himalayas. There are no modern computers here.

School Sports

Children at the Shaolin Tagou School start the day with martial arts.

Some children go to schools that specialize in a sport. These children go to the Shaolin Tagou Martial Arts School in Dengfeng, China. Over 13,000 pupils between the ages of six and 25 learn martial arts here every day. They also study regular subjects.

The school day at this Indian school begins with yoga.

These American children are practicing wheelchair racing at their school. They have specially designed sports wheelchairs. The lightweight frames and sloping wheels help them go fast.

Wheelchair racing is one of many sports for people who are differently abled.

These boys are at a school event in Bhopal, India. They are taking part in an unusual and ancient sport. It's called *mallakhamb*. It's a type of gymnastics performed with a long wooden pole or a rope.

The name "*mallakhamb*" comes from two words. "Malla" means "athlete" and "khamba" means "pole."

19

Performing at School

Drumming is a popular type of music all over the world. It's taught in many schools. These Tanzanian girls are performing at an event to celebrate Tanzania's Independence Day.

This Australian school drumming band is marching in a parade.

These girls' drums have the colors of Tanzania's flag.

These children are dressed as the Three Kings. They are giving presents to the baby Jesus.

In some Christian countries, Christmas nativity plays are traditional in schools. A nativity play follows the Bible story of Jesus's birth in a stable. Live stable animals, such as donkeys and sheep, sometimes take part in the play.

Aspara is a kind of Cambodian dance.

Schoolchildren often learn dances that are traditional in their country. These Cambodian girls are learning an ancient Cambodian dance called *Aspara*. Their graceful movements stand for characters from Cambodian legends.

Break Time!

Ball games, such as soccer, are popular at recess all over the world. Soccer is said to be played by 256 million people worldwide. Children set up soccer games for themselves on playgrounds all over the planet.

These children go to school near Nairobi, Kenya. They are playing soccer at recess.

Children are shown skipping rope in paintings from around six hundred years ago. Jump ropes are still used in playgrounds all over the world. They are a great way to play alone or with others.

This Chinese girl bends her knees to help her jump high above the jump rope.

Tig, Tap, and Dobby are all British names for the game of tag.

These British children are playing tag during a break. Tag can have different rules in different countries. They all share one important rule, though. If you're caught, you're IT!

Lunch at School

Without his porridge at school, this Somali boy might not get enough food to stay healthy.

This Somali boy has been given a bowl of porridge at lunch. He goes to school in a refugee camp in Kenya. He lost his home when war broke out in his country. His school lunch is very important for him. There isn't much food in the refugee camp.

Many children bring a lunch to school. These Burmese children carry their lunch in round, metal containers. They are called tiffin boxes. The tiffin boxes are stacked together. Each part of the box might hold a piece of bread, some rice, or stew.

Tiffin boxes are used for packed lunches all over Asia.

At this Japanese school, older students serve lunch to the younger students.

Some schools serve hot lunches cooked in the school kitchen. These Indian children from the city of Ladakh might be having stew with dumplings and a piece of bread.

Living at School

At boarding school, children live at school. These students at a Nepalese boarding school are the children of Sherpa climbers. There aren't many schools in the high mountains where the Sherpa people live. This is why Sherpa children are often sent to boarding school.

Students go to this Nepalese boarding school from a young age all the way through high school.

These girls live at the Kayaywa Tawya Buddhist monastery in Burma. Here, they learn to be Buddhist nuns. They have regular lessons, too. Most of them are orphans with no family. Their school is their full-time home.

These girls learn the teachings of Buddha.

The students at the monastery also learn to read, write, and do math.

These girls are at a boarding school in Ethiopia. They sleep on mats. They are from the Ethiopian Hamar community. There are no schools in their villages. To learn, they must travel to a town and live at school.

Nets keep mosquitoes away at night.

Surprising Schools

These Chinese children have a very unusual school. It's in a cave cut into a hillside in Shaanxi, China. Many people live in cave homes in this part of China.

There isn't room for many students in this cave classroom.

Children from local fishing families go to this school in Cambodia.

The school is the blue building. The red building is the police station.

Children row boats to school on the Tonlé Sap lake in Cambodia. They live in a floating village on the lake. Their school is on stilts above the water.

The School on Wheels is a school on a bus. It parks in different areas of Hyderabad, India. It is run for children from poor families. Without the School on Wheels, they likely wouldn't go to school at all.

The School on Wheels allows children from poor parts of India to learn reading, writing, and math.

Art Station

Here are some ideas to help you get creative and think about schools at the same time.

- Design a new building for your school. Label which lessons will be taught inside your new building.

- Invent a new school and draw it. Give it a name and an address. Make up the name of a head teacher, too.

- Design a school uniform. Label it and color it in.

- Take some photos around your school. Print them and cut them out. Then stick some of the pictures on a new piece of paper to make a collage that represents your school.

Glossary

abacus A row of beads used for counting.

air conditioning A system for sending cool air around a building.

Buddhist Someone who believes in the teachings of Buddha.

central heating A heating system in a building.

Christian People who believe in the teachings of Jesus.

community A group of people living in one area.

donation Money or items given for free.

dormitory A bedroom for several people at a boarding school.

Muslim People who believe in the religion of Islam.

refugee Someone who has lost their home and had to leave their country.

remote Far away from anywhere.

rural In the countryside.

subway An underground railway under a city.

traditional Something that has happened for a long time.

tropical An area around the middle of the world which is warm and rainy.

Further Information

Websites

Explore Japan – Schools
An in-depth look at what school is like in Japan.
web-japan.org/kidsweb/explore/schools/

Exploring Schools Around the World
Kids Discover looks at what school is like around the world.
www.kidsdiscover.com/teacher resources/schools-around-the-world/

TIME for Kids - Around the World
A comprehensive guide to how people around the world live, including what school is like.
www.timeforkids.com/around-the-world

Books

Adamson, Heather. *School in Many Cultures*. North Mankato, MN: Capstone Press, 2009.

Hughes, Susan. *Off to Class: Incredible and Usual Schools Around the World*. Toronto, Canada: Owlkids Books, 2011.

Petersen, Casey Null. *School Around the World*. New York, NY: TIME for Kids, 2011.

Index